My First Riddle

Devon & Cornwall

Edited by Charlie Fletcher

First published in Great Britain in 2010 by:

 Young **Writers**

Young Writers
Remus House
Coltsfoot Drive
Peterborough
PE2 9JX
Telephone: 01733 890066
Website: www.youngwriters.co.uk

All Rights Reserved
© Copyright Contributors 2010
SB ISBN 978-1-84924-985-0

Foreword

'My First Riddle' was a competition specifically designed for Key Stage 1 children. The simple, fun form of the riddle gives even the youngest and least confident writers the chance to become interested in poetry by giving them a framework within which to shape their ideas. As well as this it also allows older children to let their creativity flow as much as possible, encouraging the use of simile and descriptive language.

Given the young age of the entrants, we have tried to include as many poems as possible. We believe that seeing their work in print will inspire a love of reading and writing and give these young poets the confidence to develop their skills in the future.

Our defining aim at Young Writers is to foster the talent of the next generation of authors. We are proud to present this latest collection of anthologies and hope you agree that they are an excellent showcase of young writing talent.

Contents

Ashleigh CE Primary School, Barnstaple

Liam Miller (6) 1
Cullen Smith (6) 1
Kieran Whitcomb (6) 2
Drew Williams (7) 2
Lleyton Weston (6) 3
Ellie Isaac (6) 3
Ashleigh Johnson (5) 3
Joseph Place (6) 4
Charles Barrow (5) 4
Abigail Oliver (5) 5
Poppy Edmonds-Williams (6) 5
Connor Hopkins (7) 6
Jack Spearman (6) 6
Alfie Darke (7) 7
Shaunie Smith (7) 7
Gracie Miles (6) 8
Leah Edwards (5) 8
Anais Davie (5) 9
Harry Parker (5) 9
Ryan Marin (6) 10
Lexus Poole (7) 10
Tyler Roffey (5) 11
Bethan Janes (6) 11
Jasmine Severn (7) 12
Mitchell Lynch (6) 12
Jacob Webb (6) 13
Charlotte Fisher (6) 13
Alicia Scott (5) 14
Jake Saunders (5) 14
Liam Darch (5) 15
Charley Hockridge (6) 15
Jack Copplestone (7) 16
Caitlin Newby (6) 16
Kyah Scoines-Manning (6) 17

Austin Farm Community Primary School, Eggbuckland

Zak Crosley (6) 17
Ellie Durrans (7) 18
Emma Lovering (6) 18
Douglas Bailey (6) 19
Lewis Johnstone (5) 19

Lewis Alden (6) 20
Oliver Hallybone (6) 20
Chloe Milton (5) 21
Robby Pollard (6) 21

Blundell's Preparatory School, Tiverton

Hannah Al Hussaini (7) 22
Charlie Berry (7) 22
Grace Chapman (7) 23
John Bishop (7) 23
Laura Smith (7) 24
Imogen Davy (6) 24
Leo Dummett (6) 25
Emma Edwards (6) 25
Ben Robinson (6) 26
Oliver Wright (6) 26

Dunstone Primary School, Plymstock

Maddison Todd (7) 27
Tabitha Booth (6) 27
Alice Mae Johns (6) 28
Ben Hann (6) 28
Gaia Rose Bennett-Butterwick (7) 29
Mattes Witt (5) 29
Zoe Ireland (5) 30
Ethan Matthews (6) 30
Hannah Brady (6) 31
Mia Thompson (6) 31
Adam Fell (5) 32
Caitlin Newton (6) 32
Amellia Leeson (6) 33
Elliot Collins (6) 33
Robert Warmington (6) 34
Millie Chappell (5) 34
Grace Kellett (5) 34
Josie Pardon (6) 35
Phoebe Goodsell (7) 35
Samuel Nye (7) 36
Jenna Henderson (7) 36

East-the-Water Community Primary School, Bideford

Chloe Shaxton (6) 36

Grace Short (7) 37	Phoebe Bishop (7) 54
Rhys Wassall (6) 37	Darren Cochrane (7) 55
Khloe Taylor (7) 38	Leah White (7) 55
Sophie Fewings (7) 38	Emily Bryant (6) 56
Evan Squire (6) 39	Lloyd Webb (6) 56
Alex Surgeon (6) 39	Joshua Cockburn (7) 57
Paige Reeve (6) 40	Sisilia Tupou Mone Tuipulotu (6) 57
Alexandra Denford (6) 40	Manuel Sobrado (6) 58
Chloe Whiting (6) 41	
Bradley Young (6) 41	

Ilsington Primary School, Bovey Tracey

Lucy Simpson (6) 58
Victoria Squire (6) 59
Lauryn Capel (6) 59
Harry Callan (7) 60
Callum Pickford (7) 60

Fourlanesend Community Primary School, Cawsand Torpoint

Medina Tye-Kent (5) 41
Georgina Wilton (6) 42
Robert Dorrington (6) 42
Emma Beal (5) 43
Marcus Crews (6) 43
Holly Richards (6) 43

Jacobstow CP School, Bude

Sean Wooldridge (5) 61
Kate Heneghan (5) 61
Rosie Feehan (5) 62
Molly Webster (5) 62
Ziggy Zoeftig (5) 63
Tia Van der Linden (5) 63

Gulval Primary School, Gulval

Teegan Hatten (6) 44
Izzy Markham (6) 44
Jos Wearne (7) 45
Bailey Taylor (6) 45
Millie Matthews (6) 46
Isabelle Carr (7) 46
William Randall (6) 47
Joe Norways (6) 47
Isabella Davy (6) 48

Luxulyan School, Bodmin

Rory Moores (5) 64
Robin Dolan (5) 64
Thomas Higman (6) 65
Alfie Grey (5) 65
Martha Wilshaw Chanter (7) 66
Harvey Barnett (6) 66

Halberton Primary School, Tiverton

Finlay Connolly (6) 48
Amber Wilson (5) 49
Tessa Hand (6) 49
Jacob Patchett (7) 50
Russel Perryman (7) 50
Hannah Wright (6) 51
Harvey Crane (6) 51
Annabel Hand (6) 52
Max Thorne (7) 52

Preston Primary School, Torquay

Caitlin White (6) 67
Hannah Shoudjae (6) 67
Archie Cole (6) 68
George Woodcock (6) 68
Molly Campbell (7) 69
Harry Napier (6) 69
Owin Wong (7) 69
Daisy Densham (6) 70
Seren Dolman (6) 70
Zack Graham (6) 71
Oliver Latto (7) 71
Millie Johnson (6) 72
Holly Goodall (6) 72
Sasha Allfrey-Jones (7) 73

Holy Cross RC Primary School, St Judes

Rosie Tannou-Bailey (6) 53
Kate Yearling (7) 53
Aidan Gill (7) 54

Sam Waltham (6) 73
Joe Beard (6) 74

St Paul's RC Primary School, Plymouth

Sophie Williams (6) 74
Brandon Mumford (6) 75
Jack Hellyer (6) 75
Lexie Davies (7) 76
Logan Rossiter (7) 76
Layne Greenway (6) 77
Aston Jeggo (6) 77
Angel Grimes (7) 78
Luke Kerslake, Yasmin, Owen
Cameron Hardy, Jack Flynn
& Keanu Williams (6) 78

St Peter's RC Primary School, Whitleigh

Harry Moody (6) 79
Sunny Pomeroy (6) 79
Leanna Shiels (6) 80
Ella Domeney (6) 80
Andre Elsey (7) 80
Chloe Measor (6) 81
Peter Leeson (6) 81
Hannah Ramsden (7) 81
Aidan Robinson (6) 82
Lewis Bennetts (6) 82
Kayla Hodge (6) 82

The Clinton CE Primary School, Okehampton

Aiden Craker (6) 83
Charlie Roberts (7) 83
Chloe Folland (7) 84
Tom Squire (6) 84
Jamie Hancock (6) 85

Thurlestone All Saints CE Primary School, Kingsbridge

Sophie Bearblock (8) 85
Tom Newman (8) 86
Freddie Ford (7) 86
Eve Barry 87
Nicole Collard (8) 87
Georgina Barnard (8) 88
Asa Hughes (6) 88

Nye Jones (6) 89
Emma Bearblock (6) 89

Whipton Barton Infants School, Exeter

Harriet Cheeseman (7) 90
Jack Bradford (7) 90
Lauren Aitken (6) 91
Chloe Wilmot (7) 91

Willand School, Willand

Rachel Davies (5) 92
Will Sanders (5) 92
Joel Foster (5) 92
Amelia Turner (5) 93
Brionny White (5) 93
Madeline Baxter (6) 94
Oliver Simkin (5) 94
Genevieve Hooper (5) 95
Amelia Wieclawska (5) 95
Ashley Fry (5) 96
Devon Swartz (5) 96
Ryan Upham (7) 97
Shannon Grant (6) 97
Kymira Townsend (6) 98
George Hobbs (7) 98
Logan Hunt (7) 99
Lewis King (7) 99
Ellie Goodman (7) 100
Sidonie Andrews (7) 100
Kream Buddin (7) 101
Oliver van Aerle (7) 101
Olivia Tancock (6) 102
George Stark (7) 102
Bethany Edwards (7) 103
Callum Wood (7) 103
Charlotte Weeks (7) 104
Ben Cottrell (7) 104
Charlotte Crick (7) 105
Isabelle Sowden (6) 105
Chloe Phillips (6) 106
Ryan Cooper (6) 106
Yosse Mason (6) 107
Emily Vickery (6) 107
Niall Roberts (6) 108
Aaliyah Hill (6) 108
Curtis Bartram (6) 109
Asia-Mae Newton (6) 109

Mya Dunton (6) 110
Kai Clayton (6) 110
Matti Burge (6) 111
Ella-Mae Roberts (6) 111
Tilly Widdowson (6) 112
Taylor Lambert (7) 112

The Poems

My First Riddle - Devon & Cornwall

My Riddle

He is as cool as an ice cube.
He is as funny as a clown.
He is my second buddy.
He is great.
He works on Deadly 60.
He is Steve Backshall.

Liam Miller (6)
Ashleigh CE Primary School, Barnstaple

My Riddle

He is as tall as a tower.
He is as nice as Santa.
He is as fast as a car.
He is as fast as a rocket.
He is Superman.

Cullen Smith (6)
Ashleigh CE Primary School, Barnstaple

My Riddle

He is nice like Mr Lawrence.
He is fast like a car.
He is as clever as a dog.
He is as strong as a wrestler.
He is dark like the night.
He is as brave as me.
He is stealthy like a cat.
He is Batman.

Kieran Whitcomb (6)
Ashleigh CE Primary School, Barnstaple

My Riddle

She is as beautiful as a butterfly.
She is as lovely as a teddy.
She is as cute as a bunny.
She is as wonderful as a star.
She is as fit as a wrestler.
She is Barbie!

Drew Williams (7)
Ashleigh CE Primary School, Barnstaple

My First Riddle - Devon & Cornwall

My Poem

He is silly.
He is famous.
He is cool.
He is Kung Fu Panda.

Lleyton Weston (6)
Ashleigh CE Primary School, Barnstaple

My Riddle

She is as fast as a rocket.
She is as pink as a pig.
She is as funny as a clown.
She is Peppa Pig.

Ellie Isaac (6)
Ashleigh CE Primary School, Barnstaple

My Riddle

He is as cool as Horrid Henry.
He is as nice as Poppy.
He is as fit as a cheetah.
He is my friend, Sam.

Ashleigh Johnson (5)
Ashleigh CE Primary School, Barnstaple

What Am I?

I love to eat every single bug, except one.
I begin with S.
I'm the most dangerous bug in the world.
Some of me live in holes.
I'm light or dark.
I'm as dangerous as an alligator.

I am a spider.

Joseph Place (6)
Ashleigh CE Primary School, Barnstaple

My Riddle

Nice as mice,
Good as gold,
Famous as Simon Cowell,
Brave as Ben 10,
It is my friend Liam.

Charles Barrow (5)
Ashleigh CE Primary School, Barnstaple

My Riddle

She is as great as the sun.
She is as fantastic as Ellie.
She is as cool as a flower.
She is as brilliant as Poppy.
She is as funny as George.
She is Peppa Pig.

Abigail Oliver (5)
Ashleigh CE Primary School, Barnstaple

My Riddle

She is as fabulous as a butterfly.
She is as fit as a wrestler.
She is as clever as a grown-up.
She is as cool as Santa Claus.
She is as popular as the Queen.
She is as nice as pie.
She is Miley Cyrus.

Poppy Edmonds-Williams (6)
Ashleigh CE Primary School, Barnstaple

What Am I?

I live in the wild.
I love eating bananas.
I have hair that is short.
I have hands like humans.
I'm short, not tall.
I swing from trees as fast as a racing driver.

I am a monkey.

Connor Hopkins (7)
Ashleigh CE Primary School, Barnstaple

My Riddle

It is as great as Mr Lawrence.
It is as scary as a killer whale.
It is as nasty as a tiger.
It is as good as Deadly 60.
It is as dangerous as a snake.
It is a shark!

Jack Spearman (6)
Ashleigh CE Primary School, Barnstaple

My First Riddle - Devon & Cornwall

What Am I?

I am in lots of cartoons.
My type is a reptile.
I get hypnotised by special music.
Some of me can suffocate you.
I am an expert animal hunter.
I can be very camouflaged.
My body is as wriggly as a scribble.

I am a snake.

Alfie Darke (7)
Ashleigh CE Primary School, Barnstaple

What Am I?

I have legs as wrinkly as an old human being.
I am grey with a little patch of black.
I have two little eyes.
I have a white and dirty horn on my nose.

I am a rhinoceros.

Shaunie Smith (7)
Ashleigh CE Primary School, Barnstaple

What Am I?

I have got long ears.
My feet are long.
I begin with an R.
I can bounce as high as a kangaroo.

I am a rabbit.

Gracie Miles (6)
Ashleigh CE Primary School, Barnstaple

What Am I?

I have four legs.
Instead of talking I neigh.
People ride on me.
I begin with an H.
I am as fast as a cow.

Leah Edwards (5)
Ashleigh CE Primary School, Barnstaple

My First Riddle - Devon & Cornwall

What Am I?

I can play ball games.
I have four legs.
I have two horns, as sharp as a crocodile's teeth.
I walk very slowly.
I am big and heavy.

I am a rhino!

Anais Davie (5)
Ashleigh CE Primary School, Barnstaple

What Am I?

I can climb.
I can fly.
I am black.
I only come out at night.

I am a bat!

Harry Parker (5)
Ashleigh CE Primary School, Barnstaple

What Am I?

I roar really loudly.
I am big.
I am as tough as a T-rex.

I am a lion.

Ryan Marin (6)
Ashleigh CE Primary School, Barnstaple

What Am I?

I am as funny as a clown.
I come out in the daytime.
I am brown.
I live in a tree.
I swing from tree to tree.
I like eating bananas.

I am a monkey.

Lexus Poole (7)
Ashleigh CE Primary School, Barnstaple

My First Riddle - Devon & Cornwall

What Am I?

I have eight legs.
I live under the sea.
My legs help me to swim.
I can be different colours.
My arms tangle like ropes.

I am an octopus!

Tyler Roffey (5)
Ashleigh CE Primary School, Barnstaple

What Am I?

You can see me in different sizes.
I sometimes have spots.
You can see me in different colours.
My nose is as wet as water.

I am a dog.

Bethan Janes (6)
Ashleigh CE Primary School, Barnstaple

What Am I?

I swing from tree to tree.
I have two legs.
I have a long body like a snake.

I am a monkey.

Jasmine Severn (7)
Ashleigh CE Primary School, Barnstaple

What Am I?

I am cuddly.
I may live in the jungle.
I eat shoots and leaves.
I have white and black fur.

I am a panda.

Mitchell Lynch (6)
Ashleigh CE Primary School, Barnstaple

My First Riddle - Devon & Cornwall

What Am I?

I have a long tail.
I have sharp teeth like a shark.
I have a wrinkly body.
I was alive thousands of years ago.

I am a T-rex.

Jacob Webb (6)
Ashleigh CE Primary School, Barnstaple

What Am I?

I can roar.
I have fur.
I have four paws.
I have teeth as sharp as a needle.
I eat people because I like meat.

I am a lion!

Charlotte Fisher (6)
Ashleigh CE Primary School, Barnstaple

What Am I?

I begin with an S.
I am slithery and slippery.
I don't talk, I hiss.
I lay eggs.

I am a snake.

Alicia Scott (5)
Ashleigh CE Primary School, Barnstaple

What Am I?

I begin with an L.
I have 4 legs.
I roar instead of speak.
I am as furry as a leaf on a tree.

I am a lion!

Jake Saunders (5)
Ashleigh CE Primary School, Barnstaple

My First Riddle - Devon & Cornwall

What Am I?

I can walk.
I have 4 legs.
I have lots of fur.
I can roar as loud as a lion.

I am a tiger!

Liam Darch (5)
Ashleigh CE Primary School, Barnstaple

What Am I?

I am black and grey.
I can hop.
I eat carrots.
I have a hutch.

I am a rabbit!

Charley Hockridge (6)
Ashleigh CE Primary School, Barnstaple

What Am I?

I am as grey as a door handle.
My heart is really strong and as tough as a metal whiteboard.
My first letter is R.
I have 2 horns.
I have 4 legs.

I am a rhinoceros.

Jack Copplestone (7)
Ashleigh CE Primary School, Barnstaple

What Am I?

I am as lazy as a tortoise.
I have 4 legs.
I am small.
I have fur.
I hide bones.

I am a Cairn Terrier!

Caitlin Newby (6)
Ashleigh CE Primary School, Barnstaple

My First Riddle - Devon & Cornwall

What Am I?

I go swimming.
I have different coloured scales.
I lay eggs.
I live in the sea.
I am as fast as a shark.

I am a fish.

Kyah Scoines-Manning (6)
Ashleigh CE Primary School, Barnstaple

What Am I?

I live in trees.
I have a circular mouth.
I eat bananas.
I love swinging from tree to tree.
I look furry.
I am smooth.
I am very cute.
What am I?

I am a monkey.

Zak Crosley (6)
Austin Farm Community Primary School, Eggbuckland

What Am I?

I am an insect.
I have the same pattern on both wings.
You can see me on a leaf.
I have colourful wings.
I eat the nectar from the flowers.

I am a butterfly.

Ellie Durrans (7)
Austin Farm Community Primary School, Eggbuckland

Squirrel

I live in nests called dreys.
My babies are called kits.
My teeth never stop growing.
I am furry.
I eat seeds, fruit and nuts.
What am I?

I am a squirrel.

Emma Lovering (6)
Austin Farm Community Primary School, Eggbuckland

My First Riddle - Devon & Cornwall

What Am I?

I live in grass.
I have wings.
You could see me in the sky.
My favourite food is juicy leaves.
I love flying.
When I grow up I will have thousands of babies.
What am I?

A ladybird.

Douglas Bailey (6)
Austin Farm Community Primary School, Eggbuckland

What Am I?

I am yellow.
I have lots of legs.
You can see me in the grass.
I eat juicy leaves.
I will turn into a butterfly.
What am I?

Lewis Johnstone (5)
Austin Farm Community Primary School, Eggbuckland

What Am I?

I live in a house.
I have fluffy fur.
I like to eat fish.
I like to play and sleep.
I purr when I'm happy.
I am a cat.

Lewis Alden (6)
Austin Farm Community Primary School, Eggbuckland

What Am I?

I am a type of bird.
I live in the rainforest.
I have two long wings and my tail is very long.
I like to eat seeds and nuts.
I like being stroked.
I have two nice wings and feathers on my tail.
I can be trained to talk.
I am a . . .

Oliver Hallybone (6)
Austin Farm Community Primary School, Eggbuckland

My First Riddle - Devon & Cornwall

What Am I?

I am soft.
I live on the sea bed.
I eat sea bugs.
I move quite slowly.
I am like a star.
I am a . . .

Chloe Milton (5)
Austin Farm Community Primary School, Eggbuckland

What Am I?

I am a small insect.
I have brightly colourful wings.
You can see me on lots of beautiful flowers.
I eat the tasty nectar.
I have the same patterns on both of my wings.

Robby Pollard (6)
Austin Farm Community Primary School, Eggbuckland

Riddle

She is as cute as a kitten.
She is as short as my leg.
She is as plump as a koala.
She is as mischievous as a puppy.
She is as messy as a hippo.
She is as funny as a brilliant joke.
She is as cuddly as a rabbit.
She is Molly, my sister.

Hannah Al Hussaini (7)
Blundell's Preparatory School, Tiverton

Riddle

She was as jumpy as a kangaroo.
She was as fluffy as a cat.
She was as smart as a princess.
She was as pretty as a dolphin.
She was as slim as a model.
She was Tess, my dog.

Charlie Berry (7)
Blundell's Preparatory School, Tiverton

My First Riddle - Devon & Cornwall

Riddle

She is as cute as a kitten.
She is as clever as Dad.
She is as warm as me.
She is as helpful as Mum.
She is as kind as my cousin.
She is as pesky as a dog.
She is as short as my little shelf.
She is as funny as a clown.
She is as pretty as my mum.
She is as cuddly as my teddy.
She is as fun as a climbing frame.
She is as annoying as a wasp.
She is as wild as the wind.
She is Florence, my sister.

Grace Chapman (7)
Blundell's Preparatory School, Tiverton

Riddle

She is as tall as me.
She is as jolly as Santa.
She is as forgetful as my dad.
She is as greedy as a pig.
She is as noisy as a dog.
She is my cousin, Emily.

John Bishop (7)
Blundell's Preparatory School, Tiverton

Riddle

He is as annoying as Daisy.
He is as handsome as my daddy.
He is as funny as my uncle.
He is as slim as me.
He is as happy as Millie.
He is as musical as Mummy.
He is as cuddly as Grandma.
He is as clever as Daddy.
He is my brother, Kieran James Smith.

Laura Smith (7)
Blundell's Preparatory School, Tiverton

Riddle

He is as forgetful as a snowman.
He is as spotty as snow.
He climbs like a dog.
He is as funny as a mouse.
He is as good as gold.
He is my cat Zebedee.

Imogen Davy (6)
Blundell's Preparatory School, Tiverton

My First Riddle - Devon & Cornwall

Riddle

He is as big as a sheep.
He is as happy as my mum.
He is as nice as my dad.
He is as thin as my dog.
He is as kind as my cat.
He is as miserable as a cow.
He is my brother, Jack.

Leo Dummett (6)
Blundell's Preparatory School, Tiverton

Riddle

She is as cuddly as Mummy.
She is as small as a cat.
She is as smooth as silk.
She is as fluffy as my teddy.
She is crazy for carrots.
She is my rabbit, Pizza.

Emma Edwards (6)
Blundell's Preparatory School, Tiverton

Riddle

He is as black as a blackberry.
He is as orange as an orange.
He is as happy as the sun.
He is as slippery as soap.
He is a member of the shark family.
He is my fish, Edward.

Ben Robinson (6)
Blundell's Preparatory School, Tiverton

Riddle

He is as small as a mouse.
He is as happy as Mummy.
He is as smiley as Santa.
He is as bright as the sun.
He is as lively as a cat.
He is as good as gold.
He is as jolly as an elf.
He is my fish, Oscar.

Oliver Wright (6)
Blundell's Preparatory School, Tiverton

My First Riddle - Devon & Cornwall

Smarty Pants

She is as soft as my blanket.
She is as jumpy as a grasshopper.
She is as excitable as I am at Christmas.
She is as funny as SpongeBob SquarePants.
She is as kind as my mummy.
She is as friendly as my teacher.
She is as cuddly as my pillow.
She is as spotty as a domino.
She is as fat as a horse.
She is my friend Smarty Pants, the Dalmatian dog.

Maddison Todd (7)
Dunstone Primary School, Plymstock

King

He is as fierce as a tiger.
He is as shiny as bronze.
He is as fast as lightning.
He is as soft as velvet.
He is as strong as a rock.
He is Simba, the lion.

Tabitha Booth (6)
Dunstone Primary School, Plymstock

Rosie The Hedgehog

She is spiky like a porcupine.
She is as friendly as can be.
She is as cute as a puppy.
She has black beady eyes which stare at me.
She snuffles and shuffles and rolls up into a ball
She's Rosie the hedgehog.

Alice Mae Johns (6)
Dunstone Primary School, Plymstock

My Big Brother

He's as tall as a sunflower.
He's as skinny as a runner bean.
He's as hairy as an ape.
His feet are ticklish.
He's got hair like a girl.
He is Tom, my big brother.

Ben Hann (6)
Dunstone Primary School, Plymstock

My First Riddle - Devon & Cornwall

Max

He's as funny as a jester.
He's as cheeky as a monkey.
He's as jolly as Santa.
He's as fast as a cheetah.
He's as cool as a cat.
He's as bright as a star.
He's my brother, Max.

Gaia Rose Bennett-Butterwick (7)
Dunstone Primary School, Plymstock

Our Cat

She is as soft as a pillow.
She is cuddly like a teddy bear.
She is sweet like honey.
She is friendly like us.
She has fur like a bear.
She eats birds.
She is one of our cats.

Mattes Witt (5)
Dunstone Primary School, Plymstock

Who Am I Talking About?

He is as cheeky as a monkey.
He is as funny as a clown.
He is as sweet as a kitten.
He is as clever as my teacher.
He is as noisy as a motorbike roaring down the street.
He is Philip, my brother.

Zoe Ireland (5)
Dunstone Primary School, Plymstock

Family Riddle

He's as funny as a joke.
He's s quick as the wind.
He's as kind as my teacher.
He's as friendly as a puppy.
He's cheeky like my dad.
He's as sporty as a footballer.
He's as jolly as Santa.
He's my cousin, Reece.

Ethan Matthews (6)
Dunstone Primary School, Plymstock

My First Riddle - Devon & Cornwall

Under The Deep Blue Sea

It lives in the sea,
The way it moves amazes me.
It's shiny in the sun
And it's always having fun.
It whistles and clicks,
It likes to give its tail a flick.
It jumps up and down in the water.
It likes to splash in water.
It's fast as lightning
And not frightening.
It's a beautiful blue dolphin.

Hannah Brady (6)
Dunstone Primary School, Plymstock

Lovebirds

They are as pretty as a flower.
They sing like a Barbie princess.
They are joyful like a wedding.
They fly through the air and live in woods.
They are lovebirds.

Mia Thompson (6)
Dunstone Primary School, Plymstock

Wayne Rooney

He is as fast as a cheetah.
He is as strong as a bull.
He is as small as a child.
He tackles like a lion.
He dribbles like a cat.
He is Wayne Rooney.

Adam Fell (5)
Dunstone Primary School, Plymstock

My Sister

She's as kind as a hug.
She's as messy as a scribble.
She's as sweet as a bunny.
She's as annoying as a buzzing bee.
She's as helpful as a dictionary.
She's as beautiful as a flower.
She is Beth, my big sister.

Caitlin Newton (6)
Dunstone Primary School, Plymstock

My First Riddle - Devon & Cornwall

Romeo

He runs like lightning.
He is as cute as a kitten.
He is as strong as a lion.
He is warm as the sun.
His colour is like a cookie.
He eats more grass than a sheep.
He is a Shetland pony.
He is my friend, Romeo.

Amellia Leeson (6)
Dunstone Primary School, Plymstock

Who Could This Be?

He thinks he's a lion.
He sleeps like a bear.
He is as shiny as silk
And as black as the night sky.
He purrs like an engine
And eats like a horse.
That's my cat, Barney.

Elliot Collins (6)
Dunstone Primary School, Plymstock

T-Rex

He is the mightiest dinosaur in history.
He is ferocious with bone crushing teeth.
He is very tall with tiny arms.
He is a hungry carnivore.
He is the one and only T-rex.

Robert Warmington (6)
Dunstone Primary School, Plymstock

Bethan, My Babysitter

She is as funny as a circus clown.
She is as giggly as me.
She's a good listener like my daddy.
She's as playful as a cat.
She's Bethan, my babysitter.

Millie Chappell (5)
Dunstone Primary School, Plymstock

My Best Friend

She has hair, golden like sand.
Her eyes are blue like the sea.
She is as pretty as a flower.
She is my friend Eva.

Grace Kellett (5)
Dunstone Primary School, Plymstock

My First Riddle - Devon & Cornwall

As Black As The Night

She is as black as the night.
She is as fluffy as the clouds.
She jumps like a kangaroo.
She is as fast as a leopard.
She is as pretty as a butterfly.
She nibbles just like a hamster.
She is Midnight, my rabbit.

Josie Pardon (6)
Dunstone Primary School, Plymstock

My Feathered Friend

She's as white as the snow.
She wears a red hat.
She likes to escape.
She runs very fast.
She flies very high.
She helps us make pancakes.
She's Snowy, my chicken.

Phoebe Goodsell (7)
Dunstone Primary School, Plymstock

The Stig!

He is as fast as lightning.
He keeps his own secret.
He is as white as the snow.
He is the Stig.

Samuel Nye (7)
Dunstone Primary School, Plymstock

Faye

She is full of fun, kind, caring and loving.
She works in France as an excellent chef.
She is always happy, especially when she is skiing.
She is my eldest sister.

Jenna Henderson (7)
Dunstone Primary School, Plymstock

What Am I?

I am very furry and brown with a short tail.
I eat crunchy leaves and plants.
I live in a big country called Australia.
I live in an enormous hole!

I am a wombat.

Chloe Shaxton (6)
East-the-Water Community Primary School, Bideford

My First Riddle – Devon & Cornwall

What Am I?

I have long feet for jumping high.
I have a long tail and I am yellow.
I eat delicious leaves and green plants.
I live behind a prickly bush in Australia.
I hop, skip and jump high.
I have a pouch on my belly for babies.

I am a kangaroo.

Grace Short (7)
East-the-Water Community Primary School, Bideford

What Am I?

I have four short brown feet
I live in a deep hole
I am as big as a dog
I can creep slowly
I eat juicy plants and leaves.

I am a wombat.

Rhys Wassall (6)
East-the-Water Community Primary School, Bideford

What Am I?

I can jog and jump.
I have big feet.
I have a pouch.
I live in Australia.
I can jump and bump.
I have enormous feet.

I am a wallaby.

Khloe Taylor (7)
East-the-Water Community Primary School, Bideford

What Am I?

I am light brown,
I have a pouch and a black nose.
I have big fluffy ears,
I eat juicy leaves.
I live in Australia,
I can jump with my two big feet.

Sophie Fewings (7)
East-the-Water Community Primary School, Bideford

My First Riddle – Devon & Cornwall

What Am I?

I am furry.
I am as big as a duck.
I eat leaves and plants that are tasty.
I live in the bottom of a tree, in a hole.
It is dark and creepy.
What am I?

I am a wombat.

Evan Squire (6)
East-the-Water Community Primary School, Bideford

What Am I?

I eat eucalyptus leaves.
I have short ears.
I have brown fur.
What am I?

I am a koala.

Alex Surgeon (6)
East-the-Water Community Primary School, Bideford

What Am I?

I live in an enormous hole.
I eat juicy plants.
I have a brown body.
I have four legs and I can crawl slowly on land.
I am as big as a humungous dog.

I am a wombat.

Paige Reeve (6)
East-the-Water Community Primary School, Bideford

What Am I?

I can jump high.
I can hop as high as a tree.
I have a pouch.
I have a Joey
I love delicious leaves.
I can skip, hop and jump.

I am a Kangaroo.

Alexandra Denford (6)
East-the-Water Community Primary School, Bideford

My First Riddle - Devon & Cornwall

What Am I?

I have a short tail and furry ears.
I munch green leaves.
I live in the Australian bush.
What am I?

I am a koala.

Chloe Whiting (6)
East-the-Water Community Primary School, Bideford

What Am I?

I am green
I eat fish
I have sharp razor teeth.
I am a crocodile.

Bradley Young (6)
East-the-Water Community Primary School, Bideford

Untitled

She is yellow like the sun,
She is funny like a clown,
She is lovely like a party dress,
She is like a gorilla stomping through the jungle.

Medina Tye-Kent (5)
Fourlanesend Community Primary School, Cawsand Torpoint

My Friend, Tia

She is yellow like the golden, beautiful sun,
She is like a bowl of sweet strawberries,
She is like a spring morning,
She is like a sunny summer's day in Crafthole,
She is like a slippery slide,
She is like a bouncy kangaroo,
She is my friend, Tia.

Georgina Wilton (6)
Fourlanesend Community Primary School, Cawsand Torpoint

Untitled

He is as dark blue as the dark, dark sea,
He is a plateful of scrummy fish and chips,
He likes guns, but not monsters,
He is like a stripy tiger,
He is as sunny as Porthleven,
He is my friend, Marcus.

Robert Dorrington (6)
Fourlanesend Community Primary School, Cawsand Torpoint

My First Riddle - Devon & Cornwall

Untitled

She is pink like a mermaid,
She is tasty like fish and chips,
She is like a sunny day at the park.
She is my friend, Holly.

Emma Beal (5)
Fourlanesend Community Primary School, Cawsand Torpoint

Untitled

He is a brave diplodocus fighting a T-rex,
He is blue like the ocean,
He is a plateful of lemon pancakes,
He is like a day out in a dinosaur museum,
He is my friend, Rowan.

Marcus Crews (6)
Fourlanesend Community Primary School, Cawsand Torpoint

Untitled

She is as green as a beautiful mermaid,
She is a slice of Marmite bread,
She is like a day out in Fairyland,
She is a soft white puppy,
She is my friend, Daisy.

Holly Richards (6)
Fourlanesend Community Primary School, Cawsand Torpoint

Hannah Montana

She is as cool as the king who rules the world,
She is as relaxed as your cat,
She is as chasy as a firework that blasts off,
She is as beautiful as a shiny dress,
She is as smart as your teacher
She is as talented as a dolphin doing tricks,
She is better than a star,
She is Hannah Montana.

Teegan Hatten (6)
Gulval Primary School, Gulval

Hippo

She is as beautiful as a shiny flower growing her petals.
She is as fat as a large riverbank going down the river.
She is as smart as our head teacher doing his work.
She is sparkly like a diamond broken on the floor.
She is as wobbly as a wobbly jelly falling on the floor.
She is as lazy as a fat lion growling.
She is as brilliant as a cool cat purring.
She is a hippo.

Izzy Markham (6)
Gulval Primary School, Gulval

My First Riddle - Devon & Cornwall

Monkey

He is as funky as a cool dude.
He is as soft as a comfy pillow.
He is as flexible as a chick's feather.
He is as cuddly as a cat.
He is as naughty as a seagull.
He is a monkey.

Jos Wearne (7)
Gulval Primary School, Gulval

Gorilla

He is as angry as a mum when children have been naughty.
He is as fast as a cheetah having a race.
He is as cross as a tiger hunting for a deer.
He is as stompy as an elephant running around.
He is as handsome as a man going to a meeting.
He is a gorilla.

Bailey Taylor (6)
Gulval Primary School, Gulval

Peacock

It is as beautiful as a princess putting on a beautiful dress.
It is as delicate as a cup wrapped up in bubble-wrap.
It is as colourful as a rainbow being counted.
It is as posh as a swan sleeping on the lake.
It has a long neck like a giraffe.
It is a peacock.

Millie Matthews (6)
Gulval Primary School, Gulval

Hannah Montana

She is as cool as a flower with pretty petals.
She is as pretty as a rainbow in the sky.
She is as famous as a football player.
She is as beautiful as a sun shining in the sky.
She is as cool as a dancer swinging their arms.
She is as pretty as a sunflower with bright yellow petals.
She is as friendly as a horse galloping away.
She is as naughty as a pig rolling around in the mud.
She is Hannah Montana.

Isabelle Carr (7)
Gulval Primary School, Gulval

My First Riddle - Devon & Cornwall

Cheetah

He is as active as a dog.
He is as scary as a tiger.
He is as spotty as a leopard.
He has got sharp teeth like a lion.
He is as fast as Steven Gerrard.
He is as scary as a ghost haunting the house.
He is a cheetah.

William Randall (6)
Gulval Primary School, Gulval

Orang-utan

He is as mad as a lion hunting his prey.
He is as cool as a rock star on the stage.
He is as crazy as a squirrel that has gone crazy.
He is as lazy as a dad lying in the sun.
He is as cheeky as a child playing jokes on his family.
He is as furry as a horse being groomed.
He is an orang-utan.

Joe Norways (6)
Gulval Primary School, Gulval

Giraffe

He is as tall as a tree in the sun.
He is as spotty as a leopard running.
He is as slow as a turtle swimming.
He is as graceful as a zebra galloping.
He is a giraffe.

Isabella Davy (6)
Gulval Primary School, Gulval

Tom And Jerry

He is as brown as wood.
He is as blue as the sky.
He is as small as a piece of cheese.
He is as big as an elephant.
He is as funny as a clown.
He likes to chase mice.
He likes his hole in the wall.
It is Tom and Jerry.

Finlay Connolly (6)
Halberton Primary School, Tiverton

My First Riddle - Devon & Cornwall

SpongeBob

As yellow as cheese
As playful as a puppy
He has a pet snail
He lives in a pineapple
He likes to make Krabby patties
As spongy as a sponge
He is SpongeBob SquarePants.

Amber Wilson (5)
Halberton Primary School, Tiverton

Meerkat

As whiskery as a cat
As furry as a dog
As still as a statue
It's a meerkat.

Tessa Hand (6)
Halberton Primary School, Tiverton

Who Am I?

As brown as a bear
As funny as a baby
His tongue is as pink as a pig
As strong as a giant
It is Scooby-Doo.

Jacob Patchett (7)
Halberton Primary School, Tiverton

Tom And Jerry

As clever as a comic.
As funny as a pig.
As lovely as a puppy.
As silly as a light.
It is Tom and Jerry.

Russel Perryman (7)
Halberton Primary School, Tiverton

My First Riddle – Devon & Cornwall

Muddy Puppy

As muddy as a puppy
As cheeky as a monkey
As pink as a flamingo
As curly-tailed as a snail shell
As good as gold
It's a pig.

Hannah Wright (6)
Halberton Primary School, Tiverton

The Cool Nose

As cool as a dog
As wet as rain
As watery as eyes
It's a nose.

Harvey Crane (6)
Halberton Primary School, Tiverton

Shirley

As sweet as my brother asleep
As good as me
As lovely as Little Red riding Hood
As beautiful as a ring
As kind as me
It is Shirley.

Annabel Hand (6)
Halberton Primary School, Tiverton

What Is It?

As clever as a scientist
As fun as football
As silly as a cartoon
As fast as a cheetah
It is Tom and Jerry.

Max Thorne (7)
Halberton Primary School, Tiverton

My First Riddle - Devon & Cornwall

What Food Am I?

I grow on medium-sized trees.
I taste sweet or sour.
I am crunchy to eat.
I am round, red and green.
But sometimes just green.
Humans like eating me.
People make me into crumble.
What am I?

I am an apple.

Rosie Tannou-Bailey (6)
Holy Cross RC Primary School, St Judes

What Food Am I?

I grow on medium sized trees.
I am sweet and sour.
Sometimes I am crunchy.
I am round and green or red.
Humans like to eat me.
You can make me into pie
And crumble and juice.
What am I?

I am an apple.

Kate Yearling (7)
Holy Cross RC Primary School, St Judes

What Food Am I?

I am Isabella Robert's favourite food.
I grow on bushes that are very close to the ground.
I am soft and squishy and really juicy too.
I have spots all over me.
I can be eaten by people in an ice cream.
I can be made into jam.
I am bright red and healthy.
What am I?

I am a strawberry.

Aidan Gill (7)
Holy Cross RC Primary School, St Judes

What Food Am I?

I am Isabella Robert's favourite food.
I grow in warm places on small plants which are low down.
I can be sweet or juicy and sometimes squidgy.
I can be small and spotty.
I am made into ice cream, jam or milkshake.
I am eaten at Wimbledon with cream.
What am I?

I am a strawberry.

Phoebe Bishop (7)
Holy Cross RC Primary School, St Judes

My First Riddle - Devon & Cornwall

What Food Am I?

I am Isabella Roberts' favourite food.
I grow on little bushes which are near to the ground.
I like warm places such as greenhouses and Spain.
I am sweet, soft and squidgy.
I am small, red and spotty all around with juicy seeds.
I am made into jam, smoothies and a milkshake.
I'm eaten at Wimbledon.
What am I?

A strawberry.

Darren Cochrane (7)
Holy Cross RC Primary School, St Judes

What Food Am I?

I grow underground where it is dark.
I am yummy to eat with cheese and beans.
I taste different depending on how I am cooked.
I am brown all over and I can be small or large.
Nearly everyone likes to eat me.
I am made into crisps and chips.
What am I?

I am a potato.

Leah White (7)
Holy Cross RC Primary School, St Judes

What Food Am I?

I grow underground in the dark.
I am tasty with tuna.
I taste different depending on how I am cooked.
I am brown and oval shaped with marks.
I am large or small.
Nearly everyone likes me especially if I am roasted.
I am made into crisps and chips.
What am I?

I am a potato.

Emily Bryant (6)
Holy Cross RC Primary School, St Judes

What Food Am I?

I grow on trees in bunches.
I am soft and chewy.
I am curved and yellow.
You peel me to eat me.
I am a monkey's favourite food.
What am I?

A banana.

Lloyd Webb (6)
Holy Cross RC Primary School, St Judes

My First Riddle - Devon & Cornwall

What Food Am I?

I am Isabella Robert's favourite food.
I grow on small plants and in hot places such as Spain.
I'm sweet, soft, squidgy and juicy.
I'm spotty and I've got leaves on me.
Some people put me in ice cream, whipped cream
And you can make me into a smoothie.
What am I?

I am a strawberry.

Joshua Cockburn (7)
Holy Cross RC Primary School, St Judes

What Food Am I?

I grow on trees in bunches.
I am soft and chewy.
I am curved and yellow.
You peel me to eat me.
I am a monkey's favourite food.
What food am I?

I am a banana.

Sisilia Tupou Mone Tuipulotu (6)
Holy Cross RC Primary School, St Judes

What Food Am I?

I grow on trees.
I am sweet or sour.
I am crunchy.
I am round, red and green sometimes just green.
Humans like eating me.
Mummy makes me into crumble or pie.
What am I?

I am an apple.

Manuel Sobrado (6)
Holy Cross RC Primary School, St Judes

Mystery Animal Riddle

He is as cute as a small baby.
He is as cheeky as a cheetah.
He is as fluffy as my rug.
He is as white as the clouds.
He is as black as midnight.
He is as smelly as a toilet.
He is as wet as a round tank.
He is as silly as my brother.
He is as kind as my teacher.
He is as fast as a lion.
He bucks as high as a house.
He is as sweet as a butterfly.
He is as funny as a cheetah.

He is my horse Jem Jem.

Lucy Simpson (6)
Ilsington Primary School, Bovey Tracey

Mystery Animal Riddle

She is as snugly as a cushion.
She is as funny as a clown.
She is as muddy as a muddy puddle.

My horse Daisy.

Victoria Squire (6)
Ilsington Primary School, Bovey Tracey

Mystery Animal Riddle

He is as cute as a puppy,
He is as fluffy as a stuffed teddy bear,
He is as multicoloured as a rainbow,
He is as funny as a hilarious clown,
He is as tubby as a massive fish tank,
He is as fast as a laughing hyena,
He is as cuddly as my teddy bear,
He is as soft as a lovely flower,

He is my rabbit, Fluffy.

Lauryn Capel (6)
Ilsington Primary School, Bovey Tracey

Mystery Animal Riddle

He is as fun as a funfair.
He is as small as a small monkey.
He is as furry as a big duck.
He is as fast as a Lamborghini.
He is as smooth as a hammerhead shark.

He is my dog.

Harry Callan (7)
Ilsington Primary School, Bovey Tracey

Mystery Animal Riddle

He is as bumpy as a wooden fence
He is as big as an elephant
He is as smooth as tissue paper

He is my shark.

Callum Pickford (7)
Ilsington Primary School, Bovey Tracey

My First Riddle - Devon & Cornwall

My Friend Tia

She is as nice as Charley
She is as cute as a jelly bean
She is as wonderful as a puppy

She is Tia.

Sean Wooldridge (5)
Jacobstow CP School, Bude

My Dog Sammy

She is as cute as a kitten
She sits on my lap every day
She is as cuddly as a teddy bear

She is Sammy, my dog.

Kate Heneghan (5)
Jacobstow CP School, Bude

My Dog Harry

She is as black as the night sky.
She is as noisy as a gun.
She is as dirty as a sheep.
She is the cutest thing on Earth.

She is Harry, my dog.

Rosie Feehan (5)
Jacobstow CP School, Bude

My Lamb

She is as cute as a kitten.
She is as funny as a joke.
She is as dirty as a pig.
She is as curly as a caterpillar.

She is Molly, my lamb.

Molly Webster (5)
Jacobstow CP School, Bude

My First Riddle - Devon & Cornwall

My Cousin Joe

He can jump higher than a house.
He can hop over a car.
He can climb higher than a tree.
He can drive car.

He is Joe, my cousin.

Ziggy Zoeftig (5)
Jacobstow CP School, Bude

My Cousin Chloe

She swims like a dolphin.
She is as sweet as chocolate.
She is as funny as a monkey.
She is as cute as a kitten.

She is my cousin, Chloe.

Tia Van der Linden (5)
Jacobstow CP School, Bude

My First Riddle

He is as aggressive as a soldier,
He has long teeth in his jaws -
As sharp as a wolf,
He is as big as an elephant.

He is a tyrannosaurus rex.

Rory Moores (5)
Luxulyan School, Bodmin

My First Riddle

He is as big as an elephant,
He is as thin as a tiger,
He is as friendly as a friend,
He is as cuddly as a teddy bear,
He is as fast as a lion,
He is good at gardening.

He is my dad.

Robin Dolan (5)
Luxulyan School, Bodmin

My First Riddle - Devon & Cornwall

My First Riddle

He is as cute as a dolphin,
He is as wet as a pool,
He is as playful as a friend,
He is as fluffy as a teddy,
He is as small as a plant,
He is as funny as a clown,
He is as stinky as a cow,
He is as cuddly as a puppy,
He is as thin as a pin,
He is as cheeky as a monkey,
He is as black as a ball,
He is as white as a page.

He is Barney, my cat.

Thomas Higman (6)
Luxulyan School, Bodmin

My First Riddle

He is as tall as a house,
He is as kind as my mum,
He is as cuddly as a teddy bear,
He walks like a dinosaur.

He is my uncle David.

Alfie Grey (5)
Luxulyan School, Bodmin

My First Riddle

She is as smart as a fox, catching his prey,
She is as clever as a scientist, doing an experiment,
She is as blonde as Paris, standing in the wind,
She is as slim as paper, lying on a table,
She is as tall as a giraffe, eating from a tree,
She is as nice as a saint, giving money,

She is Grace, my sister.

Martha Wilshaw Chanter (7)
Luxulyan School, Bodmin

My First Riddle

He is as helpful as my friend Eli,
He is as cool as a gorilla,
He is as handsome as a prince,
He is as big as a man,
He is as kind as my friend John,
He is as fast as a monkey,
He is as strong as a lion.

He is Wayne Rooney.

Harvey Barnett (6)
Luxulyan School, Bodmin

My First Riddle – Devon & Cornwall

Snow Tiger

My sense of smell is good
I may look cute and cuddly, but you're wrong
I might eat you
So run away and never return.
I'm as scary as a vampire because I drink blood.
What am I?

Caitlin White (6)
Preston Primary School, Torquay

My Riddle

My fur is black and white
I live with my mummy
I am cuddly and I also have blue eyes
I am as soft and as cuddly as a teddy bear!
What am I?

Hannah Shoudjae (6)
Preston Primary School, Torquay

Untitled

My eyes are tiny.
I am as terrifying as a dinosaur.
When I roar I am very scary.
I lived a very long time ago.
I eat meat.
I have a scaly back.
What am I?

I am a T-rex.

Archie Cole (6)
Preston Primary School, Torquay

Untitled

I have sharp tusks
I'm as big as an elephant
I have big teeth
I have thick fur.
What am I?

George Woodcock (6)
Preston Primary School, Torquay

My First Riddle - Devon & Cornwall

Untitled

My neck is extremely long.
I eat leaves from a tall tree.
I am as tall as the sun.
What am I?

Molly Campbell (7)
Preston Primary School, Torquay

I Am . . .

I am very hairy and I've got yellow fur.
My claws are sharp
I have sharp pointy teeth.
What am I?

Harry Napier (6)
Preston Primary School, Torquay

Untitled

My skin is very scaly, smoothed and camouflaged.
Some of my friends are venomous.
People are scared of me.
I am as long as a ladder and I am very sneaky.
What am I?

Owin Wong (7)
Preston Primary School, Torquay

My Riddle

My funky blue eyes are so cute!
I live in Greta Cottage
I am as spotty as sprinkles
I am as fluffy as tissues
And I have four legs.
What am I?

Daisy Densham (6)
Preston Primary School, Torquay

My Riddle

I have brown fur.
I am as cute as a kitten.
I am as small as you.
I am so very cuddly.
My claws are sharp.
I have a collar.
My house is black.
My eyes are as brown as a tree trunk.
I am so soft.
What am I?

Seren Dolman (6)
Preston Primary School, Torquay

My First Riddle - Devon & Cornwall

My Riddle

I am as slimy as mud
And my tongue is like a fork
I'm as green as a forest
My eyes are as red as fire
My body is as long as two metres
What am I?

Zack Graham (6)
Preston Primary School, Torquay

Catfish

I have a flat face
My eyes are small
My whiskers are as thin as a piece of string
My fins are as thin as a butterfly's wings
My skin is as grey as an elephant.
What am I?

Oliver Latto (7)
Preston Primary School, Torquay

My Riddle

My eyes are as blue as the sky
I am active and playful
I am as cute and as cuddly as a kitten
I live in Burridge Road
I have four legs!
What am I?

Millie Johnson (6)
Preston Primary School, Torquay

My Riddle

My feet are orange
I live somewhere very, very cold
I have got wings, but I can't fly
I am nearly as big as a bin
There is snow instead of concrete!
What am I?

Holly Goodall (6)
Preston Primary School, Torquay

My First Riddle - Devon & Cornwall

My Riddle

My fur is yellow with black spots
I live in the rainforest
I eat meat
My camouflage is useful for pouncing on my prey
I have giant teeth that are as sharp as a needle
What am I?

Sasha Allfrey-Jones (7)
Preston Primary School, Torquay

What Am I? (An Elephant)

My eyes are as small as a tiny mouse
My ears are massive
I am as deadly as a dinosaur
My legs are big and strong
I live on a hot continent
What am I?

Sam Waltham (6)
Preston Primary School, Torquay

My Riddle (A Dragon)

I have red scales and I blow fire
When you have a flying contest I will win!
I eat mice
My eyes are red
I have a sharp point on my tail
My teeth are as spiky as knives.
What am I?

Joe Beard (6)
Preston Primary School, Torquay

Amber

She's as kind as a mummy.
She's as cute as a lamb.
She's as orange as a gingerbread man.
She's as greedy as a monkey.
She's as lovely as a rose.
She's as nice as a grandma.
She's as pretty as Hannah Montana.
She is Amber Mahoney.

Sophie Williams (6)
St Paul's RC Primary School, Plymouth

My First Riddle – Devon & Cornwall

Chloe

She's as little as a cat.
She's as cute as a cushion.
She's as beautiful as a butterfly.
She's as nice as a monkey.
She's as soft as a pillow.
She's as cute as a kitten.
She's as nice as a flower.
She's my sister, Chloe.

Brandon Mumford (6)
St Paul's RC Primary School, Plymouth

JLS Aston

He is as smart as a snooker player,
He's as cool as a football player,
He is as kind as a teacher,
He is as happy as a guinea pig,
He is as posh as Elvis Presley,
He is as helpful as a kid

The person is Aston from JLS.

Jack Hellyer (6)
St Paul's RC Primary School, Plymouth

Lexie's Riddle

He is as handsome as my dad,
He is as nice as my teacher,
He is as cool as a singer,
He is as funny as my brother,
He's as wonderful as a pop star,
He's as good as a footballer,
He's as beautiful as JLS,

He's Zac Effron.

Lexie Davies (7)
St Paul's RC Primary School, Plymouth

Sharon

She's as pretty as a butterfly.
She's as happy as a clown.
She's as kind as a king.
She's as loving as a rabbit.
She's as peaceful as the sun.
She's as helpful as a policeman.
She's as bright as the stars.

She's Sharon Lowes Hill.

Logan Rossiter (7)
St Paul's RC Primary School, Plymouth

My First Riddle - Devon & Cornwall

Untitled

He's as funny as a pig.
He's as kind as a kid.
He's as helpful as a mummy.
He's as special as a pet.
He's as happy as a butterfly.
He's as loving as a rabbit.
He's as cool as a cheetah.

It's Coby.

Layne Greenway (6)
St Paul's RC Primary School, Plymouth

He's ...

He's as funny as a clown,
As lovely as my family,
As cuddly as a guinea pig,
As beautiful as a rainbow,

He's my dog, Remey.

Aston Jeggo (6)
St Paul's RC Primary School, Plymouth

Untitled

It's as fast as a lion.
It's as fast as Road Runner.
It's as spotty as a Dalmatian.
It's as soft as a cat.

It's a cheetah.

Angel Grimes (7)
St Paul's RC Primary School, Plymouth

Untitled

She's as beautiful as a flower.
She's as kind as Snow White.
She's as helpful as Little Red Riding Hood.

She's my mummy!

**Luke Kerslake, Yasmin, Owen,
Cameron Hardy, Jack Flynn & Keanu Williams (6)**
St Paul's RC Primary School, Plymouth

My First Riddle - Devon & Cornwall

Who Am I?

He is spotty, like a spotty snail
He is as funny as a clown
He is happy, like me
He is fast, like a cheetah
He is smelly, like a frog

He is SpongeBob.

Harry Moody (6)
St Peter's RC Primary School, Whitleigh

Who Am I?

He is goofy like a baby
He is tall, like the giant from Jack and the Beanstalk
He is yellow, like the sun
He has spots as big as balls

He is SpongeBob.

Sunny Pomeroy (6)
St Peter's RC Primary School, Whitleigh

Who Am I?

He is as smiley as a chimpanzee
He is as yellow as a banana

He is SpongeBob.

Leanna Shiels (6)
St Peter's RC Primary School, Whitleigh

Who Am I?

He is funny like a clown
He is happy like a clown

He is SpongeBob.

Ella Domeney (6)
St Peter's RC Primary School, Whitleigh

Who Am I?

He is as powerful as anything
He is strong
He is a Pokémon

He is Pikachu.

Andre Elsey (7)
St Peter's RC Primary School, Whitleigh

My First Riddle – Devon & Cornwall

Who Am I?

She gets angry all the time
She is a Simpson
She is Bart and Maggie's sister

She is Lisa Simpson.

Chloe Measor (6)
St Peter's RC Primary School, Whitleigh

Who Am I?

He is lazy and fat
He is as silly as a pig
He is as empty as a bucket

He is Homer Simpson.

Peter Leeson (6)
St Peter's RC Primary School, Whitleigh

Who Am I?

She is as pretty as a peach
She is as nice as a butterfly
She is as colourful as a rainbow
She is as lovely as a rose

She is Cinderella.

Hannah Ramsden (7)
St Peter's RC Primary School, Whitleigh

Who Am I?

He is as funny as a clown
He is as good as a bee
He is as cool as Bart Simpson
He is as smart as a teacher

He is SpongeBob.

Aidan Robinson (6)
St Peter's RC Primary School, Whitleigh

Who Am I?

He is as drunk as a skunk
He is as fat as a pig
He is as lazy as a slug
He is as silly as a billy goat

He is Homer Simpson.

Lewis Bennetts (6)
St Peter's RC Primary School, Whitleigh

Who Am I?

He is as funny as a party
He is as yellow as a sea horse

He is SpongeBob.

Kayla Hodge (6)
St Peter's RC Primary School, Whitleigh

My First Riddle - Devon & Cornwall

My Friend Tom

He is as happy as a crazy clown
He is as funny as Mario
He is as nice as my teacher
He is as friendly as Batman
He is as clever as the Wii

He is my best friend Tom.

Aiden Craker (6)
The Clinton CE Primary School, Okehampton

He Is Gerrard

He is as fast as a cheetah
He is as good as my dog
He is as famous as the World Cup
He is as strong as a striker

He is Gerrard.

Charlie Roberts (7)
The Clinton CE Primary School, Okehampton

My Holiday In Turkey

It is as hot as hot chocolate
It is as nice as a bag of chocolate sweets
It is as cool as an ice cream
It is as generous as my auntie Barb
It is as beautiful as the night sky

It is Turkey.

Chloe Folland (7)
The Clinton CE Primary School, Okehampton

My Best Friend Aiden

He is as cheeky as a monkey
He is as happy as a hippo
He is as fair as the moon
He is as friendly as my brother Jack
He is as fast as Mario

He is my best friend Aiden.

Tom Squire (6)
The Clinton CE Primary School, Okehampton

My First Riddle - Devon & Cornwall

My Friend Harry

He is as funny as a clown
He is as fast as a cheetah
He is as blonde as the stars
He is as cool as Gerrard
He is as good as Robin Hood

He is my friend, Harry.

Jamie Hancock (6)
The Clinton CE Primary School, Okehampton

My Riddle

As precious as glass,
As fluffy as a pom-pom ball,
As lovely as a flower,
As furry as a kitten,
As naughty as a boy,
As tiny as a mouse,
As light as a feather,
As cuddly as a teddy bear,
As sweet as honey.
It's my pet hamster Hammy!

Sophie Bearblock (8)
Thurlestone All Saints CE Primary School, Kingsbridge

My Riddle

As iconic as Elvis Presley!
As cool as a stunt man,
As mad as a gorilla.
As out of this world as a space shuttle.
As funky as a monkey.
He has a hat, cooler than a cat!
As funny as a pop star.
He did 13 great albums.
He is Michael Jackson, the king of pop!

Tom Newman (8)
Thurlestone All Saints CE Primary School, Kingsbridge

My Riddle

He's as cute as a baby,
He's as white as a polar bear,
He's as fast as a cheetah,
He's as small as a melon,
He's as sweet as a baby gorilla,
He's as young as a seed,
He's as loud as a drum kit,
He's as springy as a spring.
It's my puppy, George!

Freddie Ford (7)
Thurlestone All Saints CE Primary School, Kingsbridge

My First Riddle - Devon & Cornwall

My Riddle

She's as funny as a clown.
She's as sparkly as a jewel,
She's as pretty as a bluebell,
She's as cool as ice cream,
She's as good as a fairy,
She's as good as the sun.
She's my best friend, Hannah!

Eve Barry
Thurlestone All Saints CE Primary School, Kingsbridge

My Riddle

She is as funny as a monkey.
She is as beautiful as a princess.
She is as lovely as a peach.
She is as friendly as a butterfly.
She is my friend Gemma.

Nicole Collard (8)
Thurlestone All Saints CE Primary School, Kingsbridge

My Riddle

As cool as a monkey.
As cute as a feather.
As nice as a cuddly toy.
As noisy as a lion.
She's my sister Emma.

Georgina Barnard (8)
Thurlestone All Saints CE Primary School, Kingsbridge

My Riddle

He's as cool as an ice cream.
He's as funny as a clown.
He's as awesome as Star Wars.
He's as clever as a cat.
He's my best friend, George!

Asa Hughes (6)
Thurlestone All Saints CE Primary School, Kingsbridge

My First Riddle - Devon & Cornwall

My Riddle

He's as mad as a monkey.
He's as cool as Mario.
He's as friendly as a frog.
He's as funny as a bunny.
He is Dan, my best friend!

Nye Jones (6)
Thurlestone All Saints CE Primary School, Kingsbridge

My Riddle

She's as pretty as a puppy.
She's as cool as a snowflake.
She's as clever as a solicitor.
She's as sweet as sugar.
She's as funny as a joke.
She's my best friend Zoe!

Emma Bearblock (6)
Thurlestone All Saints CE Primary School, Kingsbridge

Who is She?

She wears as dress with sparkles on.
She's the best singer ever.
She sings 'Butterfly Fly Away'.
When she's on stage, she's her.
When she's not, she's someone else.
She is Hannah Montana.

Harriet Cheeseman (7)
Whipton Barton Infants School, Exeter

What Are They?

You find them in a street.
They always change colour.
They have three eyes.
When they are not working they have no eyes.
They are traffic lights.

Jack Bradford (7)
Whipton Barton Infants School, Exeter

My First Riddle - Devon & Cornwall

What Am I Doing?

You use a ball in the hall.
You can throw if you're not slow.
It's a lot of fun when you go for a run.
You can play with a bat or a big mat.
What am I doing?
Sport!

Lauren Aitken (6)
Whipton Barton Infants School, Exeter

Who Are They?

They give you work
But they don't pay you.
They can be a little bit strict
But also kind.
They have a head,
They can turn red.
They are my teachers!

Chloe Wilmot (7)
Whipton Barton Infants School, Exeter

She Is . . .

She is as fluffy as a sheep.
She is as fluffy as a jumper.
She is as happy as the sun.
She is a dog.

Rachel Davies (5)
Willand School, Willand

Untitled

She is as graceful as a queen.
She is as beautiful as a rainbow.
She is as silent as a snail.
She is an owl.

Will Sanders (5)
Willand School, Willand

Untitled

He is as bouncy as a trampoline.
He is as nippy as a shark.
He is as happy as the sun.
He is a dog.

Joel Foster (5)
Willand School, Willand

My First Riddle - Devon & Cornwall

Untitled

She is as fluffy as a pillow.
She is as happy as the sun.
She is as nippy as a crab.
She is as big as a giant.
She is as friendly as our class.
She is a dog.

Amelia Turner (5)
Willand School, Willand

Untitled

She is as slow as a snail,
She is as clever as a cat,
She lives on a farm,
She makes milk for your breakfast.
She is a cow.

Brionny White (5)
Willand School, Willand

Untitled

She is as black as night.
She likes being ridden.
She has hooves.
She trots very fast.
She is a horse.

Madeline Baxter (6)
Willand School, Willand

Untitled

She is as happy as me.
She is as bouncy as a trampoline.
She is as cute as a cat.
She is as friendly as a robin.
She is a dog.

Oliver Simkin (5)
Willand School, Willand

My First Riddle - Devon & Cornwall

Untitled

She is as silent as the wind.
She is as graceful as a ballerina.
She is as beautiful as a princess.
She is as clever as a girl.
She is as speedy as a cheetah.
She is as greedy as a monster.
She is my pet owl.

Genevieve Hooper (5)
Willand School, Willand

Untitled

She is as happy as the sun.
She is as bouncy as a trampoline.
She is as fluffy as a pillow.
She is as friendly as a robin.
She is as nippy as a tiger.
She is a dog.

Amelia Wieclawska (5)
Willand School, Willand

Untitled

He is as bouncy as a frog.
He is as big as a giant.
He is as fluffy as a sheep.
He is as cute as a rabbit.
He is as nippy as a shark.
He is a dog.

Ashley Fry (5)
Willand School, Willand

He Is . . .

He is as happy as the sun.
He is as bouncy as a ball.
He is as fluffy as a bear.
He is as nippy as a crab.
He is as big as a giant.
He is a dog.

Devon Swartz (5)
Willand School, Willand

Untitled

I am as grey as the dull sky.
I am as big as an elephant.
I swim as quickly as a fish.
I live under the sea.
I eat fish or people or sea horses.
What am I?

Answer: A shark.

Ryan Upham (7)
Willand School, Willand

Untitled

I am as yellow as the sun and I am as red as blood.
I am as big as a human.
I live in Africa.
I move forwards on four legs.
My favourite food is meat.
What am I?

Answer: A lion.

Shannon Grant (6)
Willand School, Willand

Untitled

I am as brown as chocolate.
I am as yellow as the sun.
I have four legs.
I run as slowly as an elephant.
I live in the zoo and I live in the wild.
I am as tall as a house.
I am as big as a school.
I really like grass, I like leaves too.
What am I?

Answer: A giraffe.

Kymira Townsend (6)
Willand School, Willand

Slippery Secret

I can be as short as a stick and I can be as long as a log.
I can be as fast as a train and I can be as slow as a tortoise.
I can live in the forest and in the water and in the zoo.
I eat crocodiles, people and wildebeest.
I am as scaly as tiles and as green as the grass.
What am I?

Answer: A snake.

George Hobbs (7)
Willand School, Willand

My First Riddle – Devon & Cornwall

Untitled

I'm as yellow as SpongeBob.
I eat flaky food.
I am as small as a mouse.
I live in water, as clear as windows.
What am I?

Answer: A goldfish.

Logan Hunt (7)
Willand School, Willand

Untitled

I am amazing at football.
You can find me at Anfield.
I play for two teams.
I live in England.
I'm as tall as a door.
When I score I shout, 'Yeah!'
I have brown hair.
Who am I?

Answer: Fernando Torres.

Lewis King (7)
Willand School, Willand

Untitled

I'm as yellow as the sunshine.
I have brown spots
They look like brown patches of mud.
I am as tall as a house.
I am as tall as a van.
I'm as slow as a tortoise.
I'm as slow as a starfish.
You can find me in the zoo
Or maybe in the jungle.
I like eating leaves.
What am I?

Answer: A giraffe.

Ellie Goodman (7)
Willand School, Willand

Untitled

I am as brown as a bear.
I live in the smelly zoo or in the green jungle.
I crawl like an ant and I swing.
I eat juicy fruit and bananas as yellow as the sun.
What am I?

Answer: A monkey.

Sidonie Andrews (7)
Willand School, Willand

My First Riddle - Devon & Cornwall

Untitled

I can be as big as a foal.
I have four legs and I can run fast.
I live in the woods and jungles.
My favourite food is meat.
My fur has spots and is orange.
What am I?

Answer: A cheetah.

Kream Buddin (7)
Willand School, Willand

Who Am I?

I can be as red as fire, and as black as night.
I am as small as a child.
I am a famous character from the second most popular game in the world.
I have no home.
I destroy robots, save people and I'm very cool.
Who am I?

Answer: Shadow from Sonic.

Oliver van Aerle (7)
Willand School, Willand

Untitled

I can be as bumpy as chicken pox.
I can be as green as the trees.
I can be as big as a window.
I can move quickly in the water and I have four legs.
I live in the mucky swamps.
I eat people, fish or meat as juicy as oranges.
What am I?

Answer: A crocodile.

Olivia Tancock (6)
Willand School, Willand

Untitled

I am as big as a fence.
I am as big as a chair.
I am as fast as a horse.
I am as fast as a tiger.
I can live in the wild.
I will eat people, meat and chew bones.
I can be golden yellow.
What am I?

Answer: A lion.

George Stark (7)
Willand School, Willand

My First Riddle - Devon & Cornwall

What Am I?

I can be as big as a toad.
I can also be small as a guinea pig.
I can be as fast as a bike.
I can be as fast as a rabbit.
I can be as green as grass.
I can be as grey as wood.
I eat flies as juicy as apples
And beetles as black as coal.
I can live anywhere cold.
What am I?

Answer: A frog.

Bethany Edwards (7)
Willand School, Willand

What Am I?

I am as big as a ball.
I am as big as a balloon.
I can run as fast as the wind.
I've got four legs and walk like a cat.
You can see me in a pet shop.
You can see me in a kennel.
What am I?

Answer: A dog.

Callum Wood (7)
Willand School, Willand

Untitled

I can be as big as a dog or I can be as small as a puppy.
I can be as grey as a cloud or as white as the frost.
I can walk as slowly as a snail or as fast as the wind.
I can live in the pet shop or I can live in a house.
I can eat meat or fish, but fish is my favourite.
What am I?

Answer: A cat.

Charlotte Weeks (7)
Willand School, Willand

Untitled

I live in the wild or in the zoo.
I like to eat leaves and drink water.
I am as big as a house or as tall as a tree.
I am as yellow as the sun.
I have four legs and run as fast as a jet.
What am I?

Answer: A giraffe.

Ben Cottrell (7)
Willand School, Willand

Untitled

I can be as red as a sunset or as orange as a faint fire.
I can be as small as a cat, though I'm normally as big as a calf.
I have four legs and I can run as fast as a lion.
I live in places where the rocks are as big as boulders
And where the sun is as hot as a very hot oven.
I love eating rabbits as juicy as strawberries.
What am I?

Answer: A dingo.

Charlotte Crick (7)
Willand School, Willand

Untitled

She is cute, she is funny.
She is beautiful.
She has a cute tail.
She lives in the snow.
She is a polar bear.

Isabelle Sowden (6)
Willand School, Willand

Untitled

He is black and white.
He is as nice as my sister.
He lives in a jungle.
He is funny, like my dad.
He is a zebra.

Chloe Phillips (6)
Willand School, Willand

Untitled

My hair is brown as autumn leaves.
I am just over a metre tall.
I am the most talented wizard of all in the land.
I live in a scary house.
I am nice at school and at home.
Who am I?

Answer: Harry Potter.

Ryan Cooper (6)
Willand School, Willand

My First Riddle - Devon & Cornwall

Untitled

I am as brown as dirt,
I have two legs,
I flutter around,
I live in a tree,
I eat grey rats.
What am I?

Answer: An owl.

Yosse Mason (6)
Willand School, Willand

Untitled

I am as bald as a piglet.
I am under one metre tall.
I am a cartoon character.
I live in a pineapple under the deep, dark ocean.
I am as silly as Patrick.
Who am I?

Answer: SpongeBob SquarePants.

Emily Vickery (6)
Willand School, Willand

Untitled

My hair is as brown as autumn leaves.
I am just over a metre tall.
I act in films.
I live in Hogwarts.
I am really nice.
Who am I?

Answer: Harry Potter.

Niall Roberts (6)
Willand School, Willand

Untitled

My hair is as blonde as the sparkling sun.
I am as tall as a sparkling, clean car.
I am famous for singing.
I live near the beach.
I am kind and thoughtful.
Who am I?

Answer: Hannah Montana.

Aaliyah Hill (6)
Willand School, Willand

My First Riddle - Devon & Cornwall

Untitled

My hair is as brown as autumn leaves.
I am about one metre tall.
I am famous for turning into aliens.
I live in a caravan.
I behave brilliantly, sometimes.
Who am I?

Answer: Ben 10.

Curtis Bartram (6)
Willand School, Willand

Who Am I?

My hair colour is as golden as the sweet sun.
I love sweet, funny Jake.
I hate Ashley.
I fell in love with a handsome chap called Jesse.
Who am I?

Answer: Hannah Montana.

Asia-Mae Newton (6)
Willand School, Willand

Untitled

My hair is as brown as autumn leaves.
I am just over one metre tall.
I am a little bit nasty to Malfoy.
I live in a school called Hogwarts
Doing magic and defeating the bad guys.
Who am I?

Answer: Harry Potter.

Mya Dunton (6)
Willand School, Willand

Who Am I?

My hair is as black as the night.
I am ten feet tall.
I sing in a really good band.
I live in a company house.
I am really kind and popular.
Who am I?

Answer: JLS.

Kai Clayton (6)
Willand School, Willand

My First Riddle - Devon & Cornwall

Untitled

I am as green as grass.
I am as big and fat as an igloo.
I slither through the windy grass.
I live in Africa.
I eat rabbits.
Who am I?

Answer: A snake.

Matti Burge (6)
Willand School, Willand

Untitled

My hair is as brown as a tiny acorn.
I am as big as a giraffe's body.
I won the Olympics.
I live in London.
I am kind and very nice.
Who am I?

Answer: Lord Sebastian Coe.

Ella-Mae Roberts (6)
Willand School, Willand

Untitled

My hair is as brown as squidgy mud.
I am just over one metre tall.
I save people when they're in trouble.
I live in a fire station.
I am as kind as Miss Belding.
Who am I?

Answer: Fireman Sam.

Tilly Widdowson (6)
Willand School, Willand

Untitled

I can be as brown as mud or chocolate.
I can be as big as a table, although I can be as big as a gate.
I can run as fast as a car or I can walk as slow as a turtle.
I can live in a stable or a field or on a farm.
I can eat hay or green grass.
What am I?

Answer: A horse.

Taylor Lambert (7)
Willand School, Willand

My First Riddle - Devon & Cornwall

Young Writers Information

We hope you have enjoyed reading this book - and that you will continue to enjoy it in the coming years.
If you like reading and writing poetry drop us a line, or give us a call, and we'll send you a free information pack.
Alternatively if you would like to order further copies of this book or any of our other titles, then please give us a call or log onto our website at www.youngwriters.co.uk.

Young Writers Information
Remus House
Coltsfoot Drive
Peterborough
PE2 9JX
(01733) 890066